Scholastic Children's Books,
Euston House, 24 Eversholt Street,
London NW1 1DB, UK

A division of Scholastic Ltd
London ~ New York ~ Toronto ~ Sydney ~ Auckland
Mexico City ~ New Delhi ~ Hong Kong

Published in the UK by Scholastic Ltd, 2017

ISBN 978 1407 18199 8

Printed in Italy

2 4 6 8 10 9 7 5 3 1

• Additional artwork:
P14–15 copyright © Mike Phillips: from *Awful Egyptians*
P29 copyright © Philip Reeve: from *Dark Knights and Dingy Castles*
P34 copyright © Philip Reeve: from *Wicked Words*

Additional colour by:
Rob Davis, Atholl McDonald, Geri Ford

Papers used by Scholastic Children's Books are made from wood grown in sustainable forests.

www.scholastic.co.uk

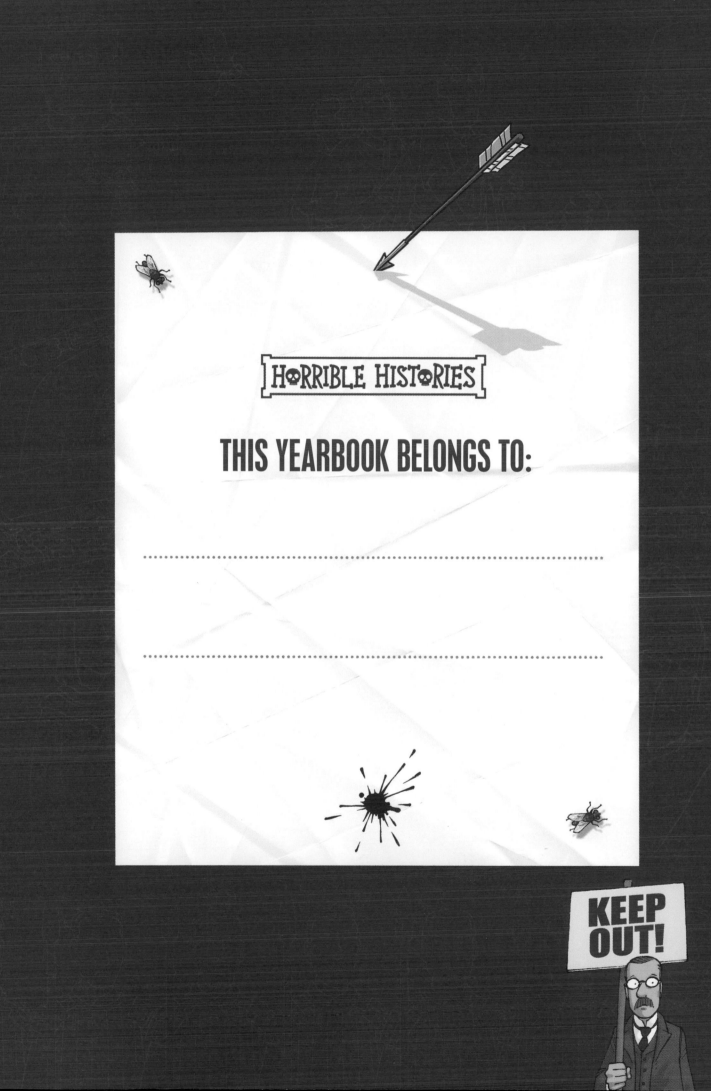

HORRIBLE HISTORIES

THIS YEARBOOK BELONGS TO:

....

....

KEEP
OUT!

CONTENTS

I NEVER KNEW THERE WAS SO MUCH IN IT!

Dearest pupils, guardians and friends of our school,

Here we are at the end of another school year. I cannot let the old year pass without looking back on the most exciting time we had. We shall never forget the day when we bought a time machine to help with our history lessons. What thrills, what spills, what disasters you lucky teachers and pupils had in the past. (At least the ones who survived and came back either alive or in one piece.) Above all what LEARNING. Here are my top four favourite memories:

ANCIENT ROME

Miss Wilson took class 4W to the Colosseum in Rome in 80 AD. The class had a good time watching Christians being thrown to the lions by the ruthless Romans. Not everyone behaved. Billy Anderson shouted to the guards that Miss Wilson was a Christian and she was thrown into the arena with just a toothbrush to defend herself. Billy has been told that we do not approve of his behaviour. NO student should be shouting at guards in that way. Speak, don't shout, is the school rule. Miss Wilson was quite upset at having to put that lion into the lion hospital. (But at least it had shiny teeth.)

VICTORIAN ENGLAND

Mr Greaves took 7G to a Victorian classroom and left them to enjoy two days with a Victorian teacher, Mistress Grimshaw. The class suffered beatings for talking — Wayne Dwayne was even flogged with a birch for breathing in class. Ellie Crosby was put in a basket and lifted to the ceiling for getting her sums wrong and Hilary Stevens was forced to kneel on rough matting for an hour because she didn't laugh at one of Mistress Grimshaw's jokes. Gary Grint was sold as a chimney sweep because he's so skinny. (This term we will be raising money to buy him back.)

GEORGIAN AUSTRALIA

Mrs Twist took 8T to Australia in 1788. They joined the First Fleet of convict ships arriving in Botany Bay and helped to set up the city

of Sydney. Class 8T learned far more from the convicts than they ever did in Mrs Twist's classes. They learned how to beg, how to rob banks, how to kidnap rich people for ransom and how to steal food for their families. They also learned how to be pickpockets. Class 8T have until the end of term to tell me which little villain pickpocketed my smartphone. (When I find out who did it they will be sent to Mistress Grimshaw's Victorian classroom for a good thrashing.)

MEDIEVAL ITALY

Mr Soames's 6S class went to Italy in 1348 where they found the Black Death was raging. Lizzie Bell wrote a lovely report for our school newspaper: *Victims had swellings in the groin and under the armpit, they spat blood. Those swellings began to ooze with blood and pus. Purple-black blotches appeared on the skin and they smelled absolutely revolting. In three days they were dead.* Mr Soames came back smelling absolutely revolting and we worried that he had brought back the Black Death. (But Eliot Walker sits at the front of Mr Soames's class and says he always smells that way.)

On our travels we met lots of other horrible people — you can read about some of them in this yearbook.

   Next year we plan trips to the French Revolution so we can learn to build our own guillotine. Then to the Atlantic Ocean in Stuart times to meet the pirate Captain Blackbeard and make our own pirate flags. Then on to Norway in the 800s to sail with the Vikings, smash monks, burn villages, capture slaves and learn how to make seagull stew.

   History has never been so much fun. Every school should have a time machine like ours.

Best wishes for the future (where we also plan to travel next term).

Terry Deary

Head Teacher

ALL ABOUT HORRIBLE YOU

What's a yearbook without a section all about horrible you? Be sure to answer as horribly as you can.

If you could live in any period in history, what period would it be?

....

Draw yourself in that period in the empty frame.

If you were a pirate, what would your pirate name be?

....

And what would you be famous for?

....

Who is your favourite person from history? Why?

....

Who do you think the most horrible person from history is? Why?

....

If you could invite any three people from the past to a party, who would you invite?

....

What is your favourite Horrible Histories book?

....

If you were going to write your own Horrible Histories book, what would it be about?

....

Design the cover for your book below.

WHO'S WHO IN HORRIBLE HISTORY?

There were some horrible people in horrible history. Meet sixteen we came across on our travels. Here are eight you probably know loads about...

CLEOPATRA VII

EGYPTIAN QUEEN
Ruled 51–30 BC
Foul fact: Cleo shared the throne of Egypt with her little brother Ptolemy XIII – he was discovered drowned. Cleo married her other little brother, Ptolemy XIV and guess what? Ptolemy was murdered. Wonder who could have arranged that?

BOUDICA

WARRIOR QUEEN
Lived around AD 30–61
Famous for ... fighting against the Roman settlers – massacred thousands of them in cold blood. Then lost. Went off and probably poisoned herself. Horrible heroine and tough old boot. May be buried under Platform 8 at King's Cross station in London. Urgh!

ALEXANDER THE GREAT

WORLD CONQUEROR
Ruled 356–323 BC
Foul fact: Alex's brother, Clitus, once saved Alex's life. Alex later had him killed with a spear. Some people even reckon he murdered his own dad so he could take the throne. Ruthless Alex died from too much wine. Someone should have warned him, 'Alexander! The grape!'

JOAN OF ARC

FRENCH SHEPHERD GIRL AND ARMY LEADER
Lived 1412–1431
Famous for ... saying an angel told her to lead the French into battle against the English. She did and she won. Then the English captured her. Joan was put on trial and burned to death – NOT as an enemy but as a 'witch'.

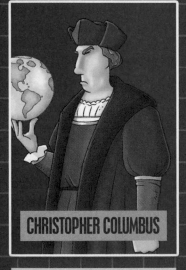

CHRISTOPHER COLUMBUS

ITALIAN EXPLORER
Lived 1451–1506
Famous for ... 'discovering' America in 1492 even though it was never lost. He thought, 'Great! All these Native Americans will make me lots of money when I sell them as slaves.' He started the evil Atlantic trade of slavery that brought misery to millions.

WILLIAM SHAKESPEARE

ENGLISH WRITER
Lived 1564–1616
Famous for ... being the greatest writer ever. At least, that's what teachers will tell you. But he certainly had problems with spelling. He was popular with Elizabethan audiences because his plays have lots of bloodthirsty murders and his comedies have lots of rude jokes.

NAPOLEON BONAPARTE

FRENCH MILITARY LEADER
Ruled 1804–1814
Foul fact: Napoleon had lots of nicknames – Boney, the Little Corporal or the Corsican Ogre, depending on whether he'd given you a medal or felled your family. Boney led thousands of young men to their deaths in war but the French still loved him. In fact they loved him so much they made him their emperor.

VICTORIA

ENGLISH QUEEN
Ruled 1837–1901
Famous for ... ruling while the British Empire grew. She was made Empress of India and reigned over one quarter of all the people in the world. When her husband, Albert, died she still made her servants lay out clean clothes for him every morning.

TEUTA

LI SHIMIN

TOMÁS DE TORQUEMADA

AMINA

ILLYRIAN QUEEN
Ruled 231–228 BC
Foul fact: Queen Teuta set out to attack cities in the Mediterranean. On the way, they came across some Roman traders and robbed them. Queen Teuta liked this idea – her ships took up piracy. The Romans sent two messengers to warn her to stop. That upset Teuta and she had the messengers murdered.

CHINESE EMPEROR
Ruled 629–649
Foul fact: a teenage terror, Li Shimin grew up to be one of China's greatest emperors. As a lad his brothers were scared he'd take their dad's throne. So he killed them (and their families) and threw his dad off the throne. The brothers were right. Dead – but right.

SPANISH TORTURER
Lived 1420–1498
Foul fact: Tomás was a monk. Peaceful enough job? No. Tomás decided Jews were dangerous people and he would torture people to discover who were good Christians and who were not. The ones who lived through the torture were usually burned.

NIGERIAN QUEEN
Lived around 1533–1610
Famous for ... fighting from the age of 16 to increase her empire. Every time Amina captured a town she found herself a new boyfriend from that town. Lucky men? Not really. After one night she had the man beheaded the next morning. A meaner Amina you cannot imagine.

CANUTE THE GREAT

WAT TYLER

MARY, QUEEN OF SCOTS

GRIGORI RASPUTIN

VIKING KING
Ruled 1016–1035
Foul fact: when the English rebelled, Canute fled back to Denmark, but on the way his army carved up the English prisoners and left them on the beaches to die. Canute returned and executed any English lord who didn't support him. He even had his own son, Eadwig, killed.

REVOLT LEADER
Lived 1341–1381
Famous for ... leading the Peasant's Revolt against the terrible taxes of the time. After murdering lots of posh people in London he was stabbed and dragged off to have his hair cut with an axe across the neck. The poor peasants lost – but not as much as Wat. Thunk!

SCOTTISH QUEEN
Lived 1542–1587
Famous for ... fighting against her Scots enemies and losing. She went to see her cousin Elizabeth I of England for safety. But Elizabeth kept her safely in prison for 19 years. When Mary plotted to escape (and kill Liz) she was executed with three messy chops. Slop!

RUSSIAN MONK
Lived 1869–1916
Foul fact: the Russian royal family thought this mad monk was wonderful and gave him more and more power. In the end he ran – and ruined – Russia. Finally his enemies murdered him – but they had to poison, shoot AND drown him.

MYSTIFYING MUMMIES

The ancient Egyptians believed in life after death. To make sure they would get to the 'afterlife' they had to stop their dead bodies from rotting. Dead rich people were cleaned and wrapped in bandages. This is called 'mummification'. Read the mad mummy-making steps below and see if you can put them in the right order.

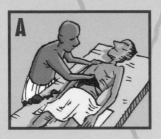

A – Rip open the front of the body, take out the insides, but leave the heart in place.

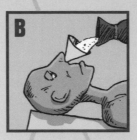

B – Throw the brains away and fill the skull with a type of salt.

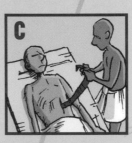

C – Stuff the empty body with rags to give it the right shape, then sew it up.

D – Take the body to a tent in the fresh air to blow away all the bad smells.

E – Wash the liver, stomach, guts and lungs in wine and put them in containers called canopic jars.

F – Put the body on a table with bars of wood so you can reach underneath to bandage it.

G – Open the mouth, or the mummy won't be able to speak or eat in the next life!

H – Soak the body in salt called natron for 70 days.

I – Wrap the body in bandages from head to toe.

J – Remove the brain through the nose with a big hook.

Answers: D, F,J, B, A, E, H, C,I, G

CRUEL CURES

It can be horrible if you are ill. But sometimes the cure is worse than the illness. Which would you rather have? The pain of toothache ... or the pain of a drill whizzing round your mouth? But you are lucky. Lucky you weren't an Egyptian. If you had a broken bone then the doctor would mix a paste and slap it on...

The Egyptian cure for toothache is so disgusting I can't even tell you what it was!

What? You REALLY want to know? Oh, very well...

HORRIBLE HISTORIES WARNING:

Do NOT read this if you are under the age of 75, suffer from nightmares or faint at the thought of blood...

That cure was written down by the Greek visitor to Egypt, Hippocrates. But he was a bit odd. He thought you could make toothpaste by crushing three mice in the head of a hare...

The 'Doctor! Doctor!' quiz

The Egyptian doctors treated people with a mixture of medicine and magic. Some may have cured but others probably killed. Look at some of the Egyptian beliefs about death and doctoring and make up your own mind.

1. In England in the 1920s people were still using an ancient Egyptian cure for children who wet the bed. What did the child have to eat?
a) A cooked mouse
b) A cooked louse
c) A crooked house

2. The Egyptians had a cure for night-blindness that modern doctors think may have worked. What did the Egyptians drink?
a) Blood from a white cat's tail
b) Juice from an ox's liver
c) Pee from a greyhound

3. The Egyptians used clever cures like onion juice (an antibiotic) and some horrible ones. In some medical scrolls the Egyptians describe how to make medicine using 19 different types of what?
a) Pee
b) Poo
c) Plum

4. The Egyptian cure for a burn was to cover it in a stuff that really worked. What was it?
a) Jam
b) Honey
c) Money

Find the answers at the back of the book.

ANCIENT GREEKS

Would you rather compete at the awful Olympics or fight to the death as a gory gladiator? Whichever way you look at it, ancient Greek and Roman sports days were a lot more exciting than the ones in schools today...

The ancient Greeks enjoyed games. Their cities battled against each other for prizes. The first Olympic Games were probably held in 776 BC ... and they could become quite gory games. If you want to run a REAL Olympics here are the rules...

OLYMPIC RULES

1 Naked men only. Women and girls are banned. They can't even watch.

2 Women who sneak in will be executed by being thrown off a cliff. Don't even think about it, girls.

3 There are running, jumping and throwing contests. Relay races with flaming torches. A sports arena is one 'stadion' long (190 metres).

4 There is chariot racing as well as music, speaking and theatre contests for the not-so-fit.

5 Winners get crowns made from wild olive branches.

6 The winners at the Isthmian games are given a crown of CELERY as a prize.

7 The winner's name will also be called out to the crowds. You'll be famous.

8 Winners get free meals for life and pay no more taxes ... ever.

9 In 'pancration' wrestling you can strangle, kick, twist and even jump up and down on your opponent. How much fun is that?

10 Cheats will be fined – you have to buy an expensive statue to the god Zeus. So cut out the cons.

Those chariot races could be deadly dangerous. The poet, Homer, described an accident...

Eumelos was thrown out of the chariot beside the wheel. The skin was ripped from the elbows, nose and mouth, and his forehead smashed in over the eyebrows. His eyes filled with tears and his powerful voice was silenced.

ANCIENT ROMANS

The rotten Romans loved a good fight. Thousands of people would come to arenas to watch gladiators fighting with swords and spears. Sometimes they battled each other, and sometimes they were up against wild animals. Here are some facts about these truly savage sports...

- The idea of fighting and killing as a game probably began at funerals. The Roman Tertullian said...

  Once upon a time, people believed that the souls of the dead were kept happy with human blood, and so, at funerals, they sacrificed prisoners of war or slaves of poor quality.

- These sacrifices changed into fights to the death between two men at the funeral. They became so popular that they were taken away from the funeral and put in a huge arena. The fighters became known as gladiators.

- In Rome there had been schools of gladiators, where a slave could train and fight for a gladiator master. If he won enough battles – and murdered enough opponents – he would win a fortune and his freedom. The greatest prize was the wooden sword, a symbol of freedom.

- When a victim fell in a battle an attendant would smack him on the head with a hammer to make sure he was dead.

- If a fighter gave up, exhausted, he could surrender. The emperor would then decide if he deserved to live or not. The crowd would usually tell him by screaming, "Mitte! Let him go!" or, "Iugula! Kill him!" The emperor would signal his decision with his thumb. Thumb down for death – thumb up for life. And we still use that sign today.

- Animals had to fight to the death, too. In AD 80 five thousand beasts were killed in one day in the colosseum of Rome.

I THINK IT'S FULL

ROTTEN ROMAN GAMES

Which of the following modern games do you think the Romans had? →

① HIDE-AND-SEEK
② TAG
③ COMPUTER GAMES
④ HOPSCOTCH
⑤ DOLLS WITH MOVING ARMS AND LEGS
⑥ LEAPFROG
⑦ KITES
⑧ BUILDING BLOCKS
⑨ SEE SAW
⑩ SWING

Roman children's games were a bit like ours ... only rottenly vicious at times! You might like to try one...

Trigon

• Next time your parents slaughter a pig for dinner, ask them for the bladder – it's a part you won't be eating anyway.
• The bladder is cleaned out, then blown up like a balloon and tied.

OOPS
TIED TIGHT
THPURP

• A triangle with sides about two metres long is drawn on the ground and a player stands at each corner of the triangle.
• The bladder-ball is passed from one player to another without it touching the ground.
• The aim of the game is to keep the bladder-ball in the air as long as possible.
• Easy? Then add two more balls so that each player has one. There is no set order for passing the ball. You may have to pass your ball while receiving two from the other players! (Game hint: it helps to have three hands.)
• If you drop a ball you lose a point. The winner is the one with the fewest drops in the time – say five minutes. (If you can't find a dead pig then use tennis balls.)

SPOT THE LOT

Answers at the back of the book

Can you spot ten differences in the second picture of this gory gladiator?

GO ON, HAVE A STAB!

19

LOST PROPERTY

one enormous wig

includes fruit ↓

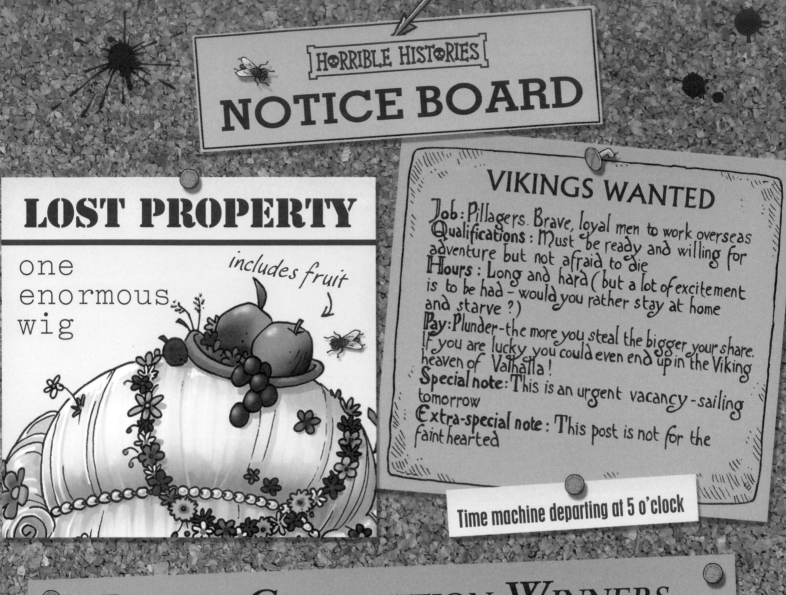

VIKINGS WANTED

Job: Pillagers. Brave, loyal men to work overseas

Qualifications: Must be ready and willing for adventure but not afraid to die

Hours: Long and hard (but a lot of excitement is to be had – would you rather stay at home and starve?)

Pay: Plunder – the more you steal the bigger your share. If you are lucky you could even end up in the Viking heaven of Valhalla!

Special note: This is an urgent vacancy – sailing tomorrow

Extra-special note: This post is not for the faint hearted

Time machine departing at 5 o'clock

POETRY COMPETITION WINNERS

1st Place

Nobody likes me, 'specially them Scots
(Me skin is all mouldy and covered in spots).
Even my own son is not very nice
(Me head is so itchy because of the lice).
Kingdom and crown, they are worth
simply nothin'
(Me eyes are as dry as the dust in a coffin).
Nightmares each night and no hair on
me head;
To tell you the truth, I'd be better off dead.

by Henry IV

2nd Place

FEAR

A terror hangs over our heads,
I scarcely dare to think
Of the awful doom that each one dreads
From which the bravest shrink.
It's not the crashing shrapnel shell,
It's not the sniper's shot,
It's not the machine-gun's burst of Hell,
These matter not a jot.
It's a far worse thing than that, son,
With which we have to grapple.
It's if we see another one
More tin of Plum and Apple.

by an unknown WWI soldier

... GET TOO ATTACHED TO THEIR PETS

THE ANCIENT EGYPTIANS
The Egyptians mummified more than their pharaohs. They mummified the pharaohs' pets and buried them in the pyramids to keep the dead kings company.

... KILL THEIR ENEMIES FOR SPORT

THE ANCIENT ROMANS
The mighty Colosseum took eight years to build and could hold 50,000 people - big as a modern sports stadium. In 300 years, half a million people and over a million wild animals died in the Colosseum 'games'. Ruthless Romans.

... INVADE A PEACEFUL VILLAGE

THE VIKINGS
In 793 whirlwinds, comets and fiery dragons were seen in the sky over northern England. Bad signs. Sure enough, the first Viking attack on Lindisfarne Priory followed. Monks were taken as slaves or thrown into the sea.

... CATCH THE PLAGUE

MEDIEVAL LONDONERS
In 1348 the plague arrived in London. Fleas carry the plague from rats to humans. Don't blame the poor little rats! They catch the plague and die too!

MOST LIKELY TO...

... ACCIDENTALLY POISON THEMSELVES

THE GEORGIANS
Georgian women used arsenic poison to make themselves look beautiful. The white powder was put on the skin to make it pale and smooth. If too much of the white poison got into your mouth you'd be pale and smooth and dead. (And it was a mistake to kiss these women! There was a scandal in Italy when over 600 men died from getting too close to wives wearing arsenic make-up!)

... MAKE A HUMAN SACRIFICE

THE AZTECS
The awful Aztecs believed they had to give their sun god human lives – thousands of them. And not only that, they had to be sacrificed in a gruesomely gory way...
They carved out their victims' hearts with an obsidian knife. Slice!

... FALL OUT WITH THE POPE

THE TUDORS
All the school history books will tell you that Henry had wanted a divorce from his first wife, Catherine of Aragon. When the Catholic Church refused to give him a divorce, he scrapped the Catholic Church, made his own church and gave himself a divorce.

... BE PARTY POOPERS

THE PURITANS
The Puritans abolished holidays and closed theatres. If you were the child of a strict Puritan then you could have started off life badly with a rotten religious name, such as Helpless, Sorry-for-sin or Lament. There was also a name for those of us who have normal names - it was 'Be-thankful'!

AWFUL AWARDS

GREATEST AT BEING GREAT:
King Alfred the Great

Alfred the Great led the first fight against the Vikings and helped make peace between them and the English. He also sorted out cheating judges and replaced them with honest ones. There is one thing that makes old Alfred not so great though. He said the only way for people to be better was to learn more - and people still believe it - so Alfred is partly to blame for you having to suffer in school.

LEAST POPULAR:
King John

King John was supposed to be the worst king England ever had. Legend says he wanted to steal the crown from Richard, and that he fought against Robin Hood to keep it. His angry barons made him sign a promise to give power to the people - this deed is known as the Magna Carta.

BEST ATTENDANCE:
Queen Elizabeth II

Queen Elizabeth II is a record holder. Not only is she Britain's longest-ruling monarch, but she's also the only monarch to have ever celebrated a Sapphire Jubilee. Marking a whopping 65 years on the throne.

WORST ATTENDANCE:
King Edward VI

Edward VI was poorly all the time. He was the son of Henry VIII's third wife, Jane Seymour. She died soon after he was born and he was sick for all of his short life. Edward died of a lung disease, tuberculosis, at the age of 15.

CREATIVE WRITING:
William Shakespeare

Shakespeare's said to be the greatest Elizabethan playwright. Although that might be because he survived longer than his fellow playwrights! Thomas Kyd wrote *The Spanish Tragedy*, which was a huge success. Unfortunately Tom died after being tortured as a Catholic spy at the age of 36. Christopher Marlowe, another successful Elizabethan playwright, died in a mysterious stabbing in 1593 aged just 29. Leaving Will to take the prize.

MOST MURDEROUS:
Genghis Khan

Genghis Khan was a ruthless raider. It's said he killed his own brother because of an argument about a dead bird. He also ordered his army to kill a million people in the town of Merv ... in a single day.

CLASS CLOWN:
King Charles II

Charles II is famous for being jolly. He was named 'The Merry Monarch' because he enjoyed himself so much. It wasn't so much fun for the people who suffered from his cruelty though. The English paid terrible taxes so Charles could have a great time.

BEST DRESSED:
Queen Elizabeth I

Lizzie was fond of elaborate clothing. She dressed in rich materials encrusted with jewels and some of her dresses could even stand up by themselves! She also tried to stay young with harsh lead make-up and chemical hair dye ... but she ended up losing her hair and teeth because of it. She had 80 wigs to cover her baldness.

BIGGEST HEARTBREAKER:
King Henry VIII

Henry VIII had SIX wives. He divorced two, beheaded two and one died. In the space of just one year (1536) Henry's first wife (Catherine of Aragon) died, his second (Anne Boleyn) was beheaded and he married his third (Jane Seymour).

FIERCEST FIGHTER:
Boudica

Boudica was one fierce and frightening gal. The Romans robbed her Iceni tribe and flogged her. So in AD 61 she gathered an army and fought back. Her tribe attacked the Roman camps and murdered the men, women and children they found there.

If you could give a prize to someone in history for their most horrible achievements, who would it be and what prize would you give them?

....

CRUEL CLASS
of 1066

1066 was a funny old year. It saw three kings in England and three great battles.

....

Name: Edward the Confessor
Ruled 1042–1066

The trouble started with King Ed. He was king of England and he promised his throne to William of Normandy. He knew Harold, head man of England, had his eye on the throne and wanted his bum on it. Mind you, Harold himself had promised the throne to William. But Edward died at the beginning of 1066 and Harold grabbed the throne.

Name: Harold II
Ruled 1066

Harold was the last Old English king. He fought William the Conqueror at the Battle of Hastings in 1066. Harold was wounded with an arrow in the eye then chopped down by Norman knights. The whole country was taken over by the Norman invaders.

Name: William I
Ruled 1066–1087

William became the last leader to conquer England when he won the Battle of Hastings. When William was crowned in London the lords all cheered. The guards outside the church thought a riot had started so they ran off in a panic and started setting fire to houses. The lords choked on smoke and ran away. Even William was shaking with fear.

Harold II

William I

Edward the Confessor

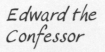

The year 1066 is supposed to be the most important date in English history. On 14 October that year, William the Conqueror met and beat King Harold of England at the Battle of Hastings. It changed English history for ever.
 You don't need reminding of the story of that day.
 You do? Oh, very well, but it's so well known you can have just enough to remind you but not the whole lot.
 Here it is with some important words missing. Replace the numbers with the correct words.

When Harold pinched the throne, William was furious. And the Pope was on William's side. 'Go and invade England with my blessing. And here is a ring with the 2 of Saint Peter for luck.'

William started to build ships and build an army to attack. But, before he could, Harold faced another invader. The Viking Harald Hardrada – and, as you know, Hardrada means tough-talking.

Hardrada was one of those Vikings who got himself into a wild state before a battle and fought like an animal – the Vikings called them 'Berserkers'. He had long 2 and a thick 3.

Harold hurried to Stamford Bridge in Yorkshire to meet Hardrada in battle. It was Hardrada who ended up with an axe in the 4. One of his Berserker friends held the bridge till an English soldier floated under it and stuck a spear up his 9.

Meanwhile William had landed at Hastings. He jumped from the ship and looked a bit of a plonker when he fell forward up to his 5 in water. (That must have washed the 2 of St Peter in the ring.) But crafty William grabbed a handful of sand, turned to his men and said, 'See how I've seized English land already?'

On 13 October 1066 Harold arrived and the battle began the next day. Harold sat on a hilltop and watched the Normans struggle to get up on tired 6. William wore the 1 of Saint Rasyphus and Saint Ravennus around his 4 for luck. But every 10 seemed to fall short. So William ordered the archers to fire higher and one struck Harold in the 7. The Normans rushed forward and hacked wounded Harold to the ground. They stripped him and cut off his 6 and 5. Finally they lopped off his 8 with a chop to the 4.

The battle was over and William was the one to get his 9 on the English throne.

Clues? You don't need clues? Oh, very well there are ten missing words - head, legs, beard, bones, arrow, bum, arms, neck, hair, eye.

Answers: 1 = bones, 2 = hair, 3 = beard, 4 = neck, 5 = arms, 6 = legs, 7 = eye, 8 = head, 9 = bum, 10 = arrow

THAT'S THE NORM!

FOUL FACT!
When Harold was hacked to pieces one of William's knights cut off Harold's naughty bits. William was furious and sent the knight back to Normandy in disgrace. 'You don't treat a noble enemy like that, mon ami,' William said.

TERRY'S TERRIBLE TIMELINE

DISCOVER AUTHOR TERRY DEARY'S TOP 25 HORRIBLE HISTORIES MEMORIES.

BHH* **1990.** Scholastic publishers invite me to write *The Father Christmas Joke Book*. It's a hit so they say...

BHH **1991.** 'Why don't we do a historical joke book?' Jokes like:

Question: Where do the French buy their guillotines?
Answer: In the chopping centre.

The publisher says, 'Put in a few odd facts as well as the jokes.' But...

BHH **1992.** I find the facts are more interesting than the jokes. I didn't know 'history' could be fun. So instead of a joke book with facts we have a fact book with jokes and...

BHH **1992.** They introduce me to a young Australian called Martin Brown and say he'll do the illustrations. (I didn't even know Australians could draw.) I write the books, Martin does the illustrations then...

1993. The publisher calls the first two books 'Horrible Histories' and they are launched (a bit like a ship only not so floaty). They sell quite well so...

1994. Another two books are produced. Then two more are ordered for 1995. I have to give up my job as the manager of an Arts Centre to be a full-time writer. (That's better than working.) Then...

1995. Book five is *Horrible Histories: Blitzed Brits* and it appears (by chance) around the 50th anniversary of the end of World War II. Lots of young readers are interested in the war and the book becomes a huge success.

1995. As I am watching a book programme on a Sunday afternoon up flashes on to the screen: 'No.1 Children's bestseller this month is *Horrible Histories: Blitzed Brits*'. I nearly fall off my chair. Then...

1996. The whole series becomes very popular and I have to write about four new titles every year to keep up with demand. They're starting to be published all over the world.

1998. People are starting to treat Horrible Histories books like proper history books and even serious museums like Chepstow and Cardiff are building Horrible Histories exhibitions.

1999. The *Daily Telegraph* newspaper recorded that Horrible Histories outsold Enid Blyton by four to one. And...

1999. A theatre director sees the Cardiff Exhibition and remembers me from my days as an actor in Wales. He invites me to write a play for his Sherman Theatre in Cardiff and *Horrible Histories: The Mad Millennium* is produced. Followed by...

2000. A smash hit Christmas play called *Horrible Histories: Crackers Christmas*. That leads to a booking to produce the same play in Barrow-in-Furness. But this time I get to act in my own play (as Rudolf the Reindeer). It's great to be back on stage.

BAH HUMBUG!

January 2000. A Schoolsnet survey showed that I was the most borrowed British author in school libraries and later that year I was awarded the Blue Peter Award for a fact book – *Horrible Histories: Rotten Romans*. (Horrible Histories are hugely popular but rarely win prizes. What a treat.)

IT'S OVERDUE!

*BHH – Before Horrible Histories

2001. Nearly ten years after writing the first book and Horrible Histories books are popular as ever. Public libraries showed I was the most borrowed author of children's non fiction in Britain – with an astonishing 17 titles in the top 20 in 2001.

2002. I get to write and perform on the ten Horrible Histories audio recordings for BBC Audiobooks where they are played on car radios all around Britain on school runs. (Parents haven't forgiven me.) Then...

2003. The Horrible Histories collection of fortnightly magazines launches in the UK and are every bit as successful as the books. And...

2006. A new series of Horrible Histories theatre plays are created with Birmingham Stage Company touring throughout the UK. They have gone on to tour the world from Sunderland to the Sydney Opera House in Australia. (More about Sunderland below.) Then...

2009. A CBBC television series started and went on to win countless awards thanks to brilliant writers and awesome actors. (I even get to play roles myself in the first three series.)

Photograph by Rory Lindsay, © Lion Television

September 2014. The book *Horrible Histories: Measly Middle Ages* was read by 426 parents and children together at Warwick Castle to set a new record for 'The Guinness Book of Records'.

March 2016. Horrible Histories keeps on finding new ways to reach its audiences. A Horrible Histories maze opens in Warwick Castle, while...

ONE AT A TIME, PLEASE!

December 2016. The Horrible Histories brand is making me a little bit of a celebrity, so in December 2016 I competed in 'Celebrity Mastermind' on BBC1 ... and won. (The prize money went to the Single Homeless Action Initiative in Durham – SHAID – charity). But...

2016. The real highlight of 2016 was *Horrible Histories: Groovy Greeks* which had been touring Britain for two years and it's my recorded voice playing Zeus. Then I discover the 40-week tour finally ends in Sunderland Empire Theatre – my home town theatre where I first appeared in 1952. I HAVE to make one last stage appearance, live on stage as Zeus, in my home theatre, in my own play. Marvellous. Also in 2016...

2016. I complete the Great North Run (a 13.1 mile half-marathon) wearing a T-shirt with Horrible Histories printed on it. Thousands of people line the route to cheer on the Horrible Histories name. But...

2017 (and always). My TOP, top moment of 25 years as the Horrible Histories writer? The wonderful readers. Without readers there would be no Horrible Histories. I've had so many fabulous fan letters from readers like a 10-year-old boy who said, 'I do not like reading very much and my mum is pleased that I have found some books I like so much that I read them without being asked!' Thank you to every single reader.

Terry thinking about his next book ↘

KNIGHT SCHOOL

From about the age of seven the sons of Norman lords and knights would train to be knights every afternoon. Good fun, eh? Riding and charging at targets (quintains) with your lance. Swordfighting and murdering little rabbits and dear deer on hunting expeditions. Great fun!

Now the bad news. Your mornings would be spent in lessons. The castle clerks were there to keep the lords' records and keep their money right. But they also had the job of teaching you young knights your lessons. These lessons were in lovely Latin! Yeuch!

And you don't need me to tell you what 'NIL DESPERANDUM AUSPICE DEO' means, do you? You do? Oh, very well. It means, 'Don't despair, have faith in God.' Write it on your next SATs paper and maybe God will give you a helping hand. The Normans wrote their legal papers in Latin and (when you grew up) you'd have to put your seal on these so it helped if you knew what they meant.

And the really bad news ... each clerk-teacher was armed with a stout stick. No, this wasn't to help him point at the blackboard. It was to whack you across the shoulders if you weren't trying hard enough. And, as a tough little trainee knight you must never cry ... or even show that it hurt you!

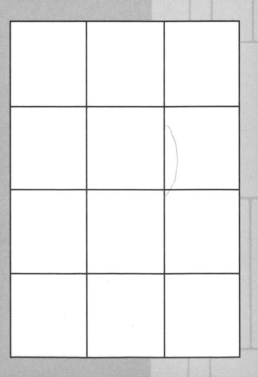

Now have a go at copying this nasty knight into the squares.

Odd Orders

Clubs for knights were called 'Orders' and were a bit like after school clubs – you all had the same meeting time, the same ideas and you did fun things together ... like half killing each other in play-fights. One of the most famous orders is the Order of the Garter. The story goes that a countess dropped her silk garter while dancing and, to save her embarrassment, the king put it on. It's now a great honour to be one of the 25 Knights of the Garter ... but just in case you're not picked, why not make up your own Order and knight your friends. To give you some ideas, here are a few other Orders from Europe...

The Order of the Golden Fleece, founded 1430

A French copy-cat called Philip the Good didn't want a garter, so he founded his own Order, the 'Order of the Golden Fleece'. There is no story of him dancing with a golden sheep so the Order of the Golden Fleece is pretty boring ... unless you would care to make up a story? The members wear a golden sheep around their neck. (No, a model sheep, not a dead ram, you fool.)

The Order of the Elephant, founded 1478

And how would you explain Danish knights having an 'Order of the Elephant'? Maybe this is for people who never forget! Or maybe it's for people with a thick skin. Or for people who spend the weekend tearing down trees with their noses. Luckily they don't have to wear an elephant round their necks.

The Order of the Thistle, founded 1687

The Scottish 'Order of the Thistle' is for 16 people and the Royal Family. They have a nice Latin motto suitable for teachers,

football hooligans and Rottweiler dogs: *Nemo me impune lacessit.* Of course you don't need me to tell you what that means ... but I will anyway. It means, 'No one hurts me and gets away with it.'

The Order of the Bath, founded between 1399 and 1413

This British Order was almost forgotten until George I dug it up and dusted it off in 1725. The motto is: *Tria juncta in uno*, which means 'Three in One'. Three what in one? Three men in the bath? Must be a pretty big bath! And in 1971 the Queen allowed women into the order. She must believe in mixed bathing. Would you want to get in the water after they'd been in it?

So what Order would you like to invent?

Name of order:

....

....

Motto:

....

....

CLASS OF 1485–1603

The Tudors were a family who ruled England, and poked their noses into the rest of Great Britain, from 1485 until 1603. The grandfather was Henry VII, his son was Henry VIII and the grandchildren were Edward VI, Mary I and Elizabeth I.

Six rulers and 118 years that changed the lives of the English people. Read on to find out who was who...

HENRY VII

REIGNED: 1485–1509
MARRIED: Elizabeth of York
FOUL FACT: Henry was mean with his money. The gossips in the palace said the Queen had to borrow money from her servants.

HENRY VIII

REIGNED: 1509–1547
MARRIED: Six times! Catherine of Aragon, Anne Boleyn, Jane Seymour, Anne of Cleves, Catherine Howard and Catherine Parr.
FOUL FACT: Henry reigned for 38 torturing Tudor years and, in that time, about 72,000 people were executed. That's about five every day.

EDWARD VI

REIGNED: 1547–1553
MARRIED: No one – he died at age 15, which didn't give him a lot of time.
FOUL FACT: in Edward's last days, his fingers turned black and dropped off and his hair fell out. Yeugh!

LADY JANE GREY

REIGNED: 1553
MARRIED: Lord Guildford Dudley
FOUL FACT: Jane was queen for just nine days before she was arrested by Mary I and executed.

MARY I

REIGNED: 1553–1558
MARRIED: King Philip of Spain
FOUL FACT: before she was queen, Catholic Mary pretended she wouldn't harm any Protestants. She lied! She killed over 300 once she was in charge.

ELIZABETH I

REIGNED: 1558–1603
MARRIED: No one
FOUL FACT: after imprisoning her for 18 years, Elizabeth signed an order for her cousin, Mary Queen of Scots, to be executed. Not a close family then!

TERRIFYING
TUDOR TIMELINE

The Wars of the Roses in England came to a bloody end when Welsh Prince Henry Tudor defeated Richard III in battle. He made himself King Henry VII of England, the first of the terrible Tudors.

1485
Richard III is hacked to death at the Battle of Bosworth Field. His Welsh opponent, Henry Tudor, is crowned Henry VII. This man is ruthless – but not utheless. He will make England rich.

1503
James IV of Scotland marries Margaret – Henry VII's daughter from England. That should unite the nations. Fat chance.

1520
Henry VIII sends some soldiers to tame the 'wild Irish' – the ones outside the Dublin 'Pale' – but Henry's too busy fighting the Scots, the French and various popes to get very far.

1534
Henry doesn't like being told what to do by the head of the Catholic Church, the Pope. Henry wants a divorce – Pope says, 'No.' Henry says, 'Right! I'll make my own Church of England and give myself a divorce.' This new 'Protestant' religion will cause untold misery in its struggle against the old Catholic Church. And English will kill and torture English, of course.

1536
Henry VIII makes Wales part of England with the 'Act of Union'. Henry's family was Welsh, of course, so this was not a very friendly thing for him to do. In the same year he has wife Anne Boleyn beheaded – so he's not a very friendly man after all.

1542
Scottish James V's troops lose to the English at Solway Moss and he dies of a broken heart. His six-day-old daughter, Mary Queen of Scots, takes the crown (even though it's too big for her).

1567
Mary Queen of Scots is thrown off the throne and flees to England. She asks cousin Queen Elizabeth I of England to protect her. Liz 'protects' Mary for 19 years in prison! In Scotland her 13-month-old son, James VI, becomes king.

1587
Elizabeth I finally decides to execute Mary Queen of Scots for plotting to overthrow her. Liz says sorry to James, so that's all right.

1588
The Spanish Armada attacks England – and loses. Spanish survivors are shipwrecked in Ireland. They are mostly massacred ... by their friends, the 'wild Irish' peasants! The English won't get out of Ireland but haven't the power to crush it entirely. As Liz's governor says, 'I have often wished Ireland could be sunk in the sea.' Charming!

WHERE'S RATTUS?

Can you find Rattus and fourteen of his ratty friends in this Tudor scene? You'll need your sharpest spotting skills! Circle each rat once you've found it. The answers are at the back of the book.

WICKED WORDS

William Shakespeare wrote poems and plays from about 1590 till 1616 ... then he stopped because he died and that made it a bit difficult. Will used 17,677 different words in his writing ... someone, with nothing better to do, counted them! He also invented lots of phrases that we still use today. Look at the phrases below and decide if you think each one was used first by Shakespeare. Write the phrase in the 'True' column if you think it was, and in the 'False' column if you think it wasn't.

• AS COOL AS A CUCUMBER • SPILL THE BEANS • SEND HIM PACKING • AS DEAD AS A DOORNAIL
• A SORRY SIGHT • LOVE IS BLIND • IN A PICKLE • BITE THE DUST • BOB'S YOUR UNCLE

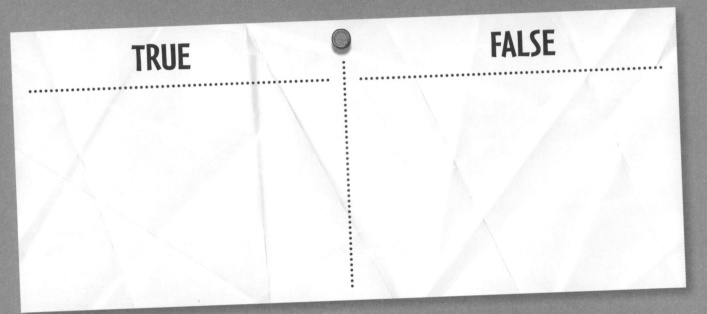

TRUE   **FALSE**

The other odd thing (that teachers will bore you with) is that he wrote most of his plays in a sort of poetry that didn't usually rhyme – but it did have a regular rhythm that went: ·············▶

So, in Shakespeare's famous play *Romeo and Juliet*, for example, Romeo recites:

AH SHE DOTH TEACH THE TORCHES TO BURN BRIGHT.

But people didn't pay their pennies to learn a bunch of new words or hear a bunch of actors go, 'di-dahh, di-dahh, di-dahh, di-dahh, di-dahh.' No. They went along to see the characters murder each other, shed buckets of stage-blood and even eat each other!

Answers: TRUE: As dead as a doornail, Love is blind, In a pickle, A sorry sight, Send him packing
FALSE: As cool as a cucumber, Spill the beans, Bite the dust, Bob's your uncle

PAINFUL PLAYS

Shakespeare's bloodiest play of all was Macbeth. Here's a short extract to show how brilliant – and how totally tasteless – Will Shakespeare could be. Warning: this play contains scenes of violence that some people may find upsetting.

MACBETH
by William Shakespeare and A.N. Other

IMPORTANT NOTE: All the words in italics in this script were written by Shakespeare (honest!). All the words written in normal type are by A.N. Other.

Scene 4 Macduff's castle

Narrator: Macbeth was a nasty man who killed the king and took his throne. Then he set out to kill his other enemies ... especially the noble Macduff. First he sent a couple of murderers to Macduff's castle...

Murderer: *Where is your husband?*

Lady Macduff: *In no such place as thou may find him.*

Murderer: *He is a traitor.*

Young Macduff: *Thou liest, thou shag-haired villain!*

Murderer: *What, you egg!*
(And the murderer stabs young Macduff)

Young Macduff: *He has killed me, mother.* (Yes. This line really is in the printed play. But it's hard to believe witty Will really wrote it.) *Run away, I pray you!*
(Lady Macduff runs away, chased by the murderer. Screams off stage tell us that he's caught her.)

Lady Macduff: Help! They've caught me! Ouch!

Narrator: When Macduff heard about his family's death, he came back home to Scotland for revenge! Macbeth was left to face Macduff alone...
(Macduff enters waving a sword)

Macduff: *Tyrant, show thy face!*

Macbeth: *Of all men else I have avoided thee, My soul is too much charged with blood of thine.*

Macduff: *I have no words;*
My voice is in my sword.
(They fight and Macduff kills Macbeth)

Narrator: And so Macduff killed Macbeth.

Macbeth: I guess that serves me right.

Macduff: So, that's the end of rotten old Macbeth. And now it's to the pub to celebrate!

Narrator: THE END!

See if you can match up the historical figures below with their dream prom dates.

ROTTEN PROM

A. CLEOPATRA

Cleo shared the throne of Egypt with her little brother, Ptolemy XIII. After she met this top Roman ruler she didn't need little brother — and little brother was discovered drowned. Who do you think her date was?

B. QUEEN MARY II

Mary II became joint sovereign with this handsome lad after her dad ran away to France in 1688. Who was the lucky man?

C. QUEEN VICTORIA

Queen Victoria fell in love with her cousin at first sight. She liked him so much that she proposed to him. From her description below, can you tell who her ideal date was?

He is really quite charming, and so excessively handsome, such beautiful blue eyes, an exquisite nose, and such a pretty mouth with delicate moustachios and slight but very slight whiskers; a beautiful figure, broad in the shoulders and a fine waist.

I. WILLIAM III (WILLIAM OF ORANGE)

William was small. His date was large. She didn't take his arm when they walked together. Instead he took her arm. Someone once said that 'he hung on her arm like a bracelet.'

2. JULIUS CAESAR

Sadly for this pair, the relationship didn't last. Caeser came to a sticky end — he was stabbed to death by the posh Romans — so his date moved on to Roman general Mark Antony.

3. PRINCE ALBERT

When Albert died in 1861 his date became a changed woman. She refused for many years to appear in public. Then, when she did, she insisted on wearing her black widow's bonnet and not a crown.

Answers: A)2, B)1, C)3

FOUL FASHION

Take a look at these top style tips from history to help get you that extra special look for prom*.

INCAS

Try soaking your hair in a bucket of wee that's been brewing for a week. This will get rid of the grease and leave your hair lovely and shiny — honest!

Hold your hair in place with — yep, you guessed it — more pee. Try first with braids; it's better than hair spray.

TUDORS

Try hiding marks on your skin with Elizabeth I's top method. She whitened her skin and hid her scars with a mixture of egg, powdered eggshells, poppy seeds and white lead.

If your hair starts to thin from all the lead poisoning, not to worry. Cover it up with a wig.

GEORGIANS

Using red plaster of Paris on your lips will make them bright red. Just ignore the chalky taste.

Try shaving your eyebrows and replacing them with false eyebrows made from mouse skin.

GORGEOUS GEORGIAN FASHIONS

Georgian fashions were over the top and extravagant. Georgian women often wore huge hairpieces that reached the ceiling — decorating them with anything from flowers to feathers. They also wore big dresses with wide, hooped petticoats. These dresses came into fashion in 1710 and went out of fashion in 1780. A writer complained that when one young lady walked down the street she took up the full width of the pavement wearing one.

It's easy to poke fun at Georgian women, but the men were just as bad. They were known as *fops*, meaning *posers* (and other ruder words!). From 1660 until 1760 men wore wigs – even when they weren't bald! These wigs could be very expensive so they were often stolen. Thieves would ride on the back of a carriage, carefully cut a hole through the back, snatch a wig off the passenger and jump off.

Now have a go at designing your own horrible hairpiece to go on this gorgeous Georgian lady.

Georgian wigs were often nasty, filthy things, so don't forget to add some loathsome lice jumping about. Yeuch!

Make sure you add plenty of decorations to your lady's hairpiece. This could include ribbons, feathers, fruit or even model ships.

DIRE DINNERS

School dinners can be dire. But at least you've got dinner. And you rarely have to go out and catch it for yourself. Or worry there might be living things lurking in it. (Well, hopefully not.)

Take a look at these dire dinners from history... They ought to make your school dinner look a bit more appetising.

Stone Age Snacks

Stone Age humans couldn't queue up in their school canteen for a freshly cooked meal. Everything they ate had to be found or caught. If they wanted it cooked then they had to do it themselves.

By studying hunter-gatherer people who are alive today, historians have come up with a rough idea of how early Stone Age people brewed up breakfast, lapped up lunch, tucked into tea or scoffed their supper.

dinner lady

Tasty tips for hungry house-
husbands and weary wives

You will need:
x dead animals - enough to feed the family
x a stone knife
x a flint to strike a light and wood for a fire

Methods:
1. Catch a bird or animal. (Handy hint: hang around beasts of prey like lions. Wait till they've eaten their fill and take what's left - but make sure they don't make a snack of you!)
2. Light the fire and build it up to a good blaze. (Handy hint: once you've got a fire going it is a good idea to try and keep it going until you need it again.)

3. Throw the dead animal on to the fire and scorch it till the fur (or feathers) burns off and the skin is crisp.
4. Pull the animal off the fire, slit it open, take out the guts and throw them away.
5. Tear off flesh and share it round the family. The meat will still be raw and bloody, but don't worry, that makes it all the tastier.
6. Serve with fresh water.

You may like to have a Stone Age dinner in the school canteen! Dinner ladies could prepare the food in Stone Age fashion and you can try to spot the difference. And don't forget your manners...

Early Stone Age Table Manners

Gorging Georgians

You'd probably prefer your school dinner to some of these gorgeous Georgian foods...

1 Daniel Defoe, the author of *Robinson Crusoe*, described his visit to Stilton, the town famous for its cheese...

The cheese is brought to the table with the mites or maggots round it so thick that they bring a spoon with them to eat the mites with, as you do the cheese.

2 When a scientist took a close look at pepper he discovered that there was more in it than peppercorns. There was also the sweepings from the floors of the store-rooms. Mice and rat droppings would be ground up with the pepper-powder.

3 Milk was sold on the streets of cities by milk maids who carried it round in open pails. The trouble was the pails collected extras on their journey. Tobias Smollett described them...

"Dirty water thrown from windows, spittle, snot and tobacco squirts from passersby, spatterings from coach wheels, dirt and trash chucked into it by roguish boys for the joke's sake, the spewings of infants and finally the lice that drop from the rags of the nasty drab woman that sells this precious mixture."

Clever Cooks

Not all food from history is horrible though. Here are some Georgian inventions that made life tastier.

1 **Tasty toast:** a nasty Swedish visitor said the English invented toast because their houses were too chilly to spread butter on cold bread!

2 **Super sandwiches:** in 1760 John Montague, the fourth Earl of Sandwich, was playing cards and didn't want to stop for dinner. He ordered his meat between two pieces of bread so he could eat it while he played. Everyone copied him and asked for 'A beef as-eaten-by-the-fourth-Earl-of-Sandwich, please.' (The Romans had this idea more than 1,000 years before, but you don't eat a jam julius caesar. You eat a sandwich.)

3 **Fab fruits:** the Georgians started to eat raw fruit. In earlier times doctors had said that eating fruit could spread the plague! With new 'hot houses' the Georgians could grow their own exotic fruits, like grapes and pineapples.

Fatten up your friends

William Verral wrote a recipe book called *The Cook's Paradise*. You can invite your friends to try this simple recipe and we're pretty certain that it won't kill them. They may even enjoy it and invite you to share their next school dinner with you.

Strawberry fritters

You need:
450 g large strawberries (more if you have a lot of friends)
175 g plain flour
50 g caster sugar
2 teaspoons grated nutmeg
2 eggs
225 ml single cream
lard (you can use margarine though the Georgians hadn't invented it)

Method: Start this at least two hours before your guests arrive.

1 Wash and dry the strawberries but leave the stalks on so you can hold them when you eat them.

2 Mix the flour, nutmeg and sugar in a bowl.

3 Beat the eggs, stir in the cream and slowly stir the mixture into the flour and sugar.

4 Leave this batter to stand for two hours.

5 Heat some lard in a frying pan. (It's best to get an adult to do this. If anyone's going to get burned it may as well be an adult rather than you. Adults are also useful for washing up your mess afterwards .)

6 Dip each strawberry in the batter – holding it by the stalk.

7 Drop a few strawberries into the hot lard and fry them gently till they are golden brown.

8 Drain them on a kitchen towel and keep them warm in an oven while you cook the rest.

9 Eat the strawberries but not the stalks.

10 If you like them then share them with your friends. If you absolutely adore them then scoff the lot, describe the taste to your friends ... and tell them to cook their own.

VILE VILLAINS
The Naughty List

'History' isn't horrible. It's 'people' that are horrible. Yet the evil men and women are usually remembered – the great and the good are often forgotten. How unfair is that? But that's history. The world just seems to love villains. And I've heard that Horrible Histories readers do too. So who were a few of the worst to make it into the naughty list? Here are sixteen of the foulest – but there are probably enough to fill sixteen MILLION books.

KING HEROD THE GREAT
Judean King, 73–4 BC
Known for: King Herod reigned for 37 years. His last years were a reign of terror. He heard that a baby had been born who would become King of the Jews. He didn't know WHICH baby. So Herod decided to think BIG. 'Easy. We simply kill ALL the baby boys aged 2 or under in Bethlehem. Off you go. Chop! Chop!'

EMPEROR DOMITIAN OF ROME
Roman emperor, AD 51–96
Wicked ways: Emperor Titus said, 'When I die I want my brother Domitian to take my throne.' Then Titus died. Doctors said he died of a fever but the gossips said it was poison. Would you poison your big brother to get his fortune? (Better not answer that.)

ABU AL-'ABBAS AS-SAFFAH
Mesopotamian ruler, 722–754
Known for: Abu Al's nickname was 'shredder of blood'. Would you have dinner with this man? His enemies did. He massacred them, then went on with dinner – over their dead bodies.

TAMERLANE THE GREAT
Mongol warrior, 1336–1405
Wicked ways: Tamerlane enjoyed conquering new lands – and then having the odd massacre of the conquered people – 80,000 died in Delhi, India. He also once executed 100,000 prisoners because it was too much trouble to guard them and feed them. His favourite building was a tower made from the 100,000 skulls of his victims.

ATTILA THE HUN
Leader of the Huns, AD 406–453
Wicked ways: Attila was just 140 cm tall but a tiny terror. He smashed the Romans and anyone else who got in his way. He massacred a city full of people to teach his enemies a lesson. Terrible tales were told of him eating human flesh.

WU ZHAO
Empress of China, 624–705
Wicked ways: she started out as one of the emperor's many wives. But Wu Zhao decided she wanted to rule the whole country. She knew she had to get rid of hubby's other wives – have them murdered or thrown into jail. So first she killed her own baby ... and blamed it on Empress Wang. The emperor believed her and let her execute the innocent empress. She had her hands and feet cut off ... then had her drowned in a barrel of wine.

BASIL BULGAROCTONUS
Byzantine emperor, 958–1025
Known for: Basil got the name Bulgaroctonus because of his savage attack. It means 'Slayer of the Bulgars'. In 1014 he attacked and blinded the whole Bulgar army ... this was not just one or two leaders. Bas thought BIG. He blinded every enemy soldier, EXCEPT he left one eye to every 100th man, so that the other 15,000 soldiers might be led back to their king, Samuel. Sad Sam died of shock two days after seeing this terrible spectacle. The blinded Bulgar army would never go home to be teachers – no pupils, you see?

VLAD THE IMPALER
Ruler of Wallachia, 1431–1476
Wicked ways: the real 'Count Dracula' was even more vicious than the vampire in the stories. Vlad used to take his prisoners of war and stick each of them on top of a sharpened pole. The poles were then arranged around his camp and he enjoyed a tasty dinner while the victims screamed and died all around him. Something to liven up school dinners, perhaps?

PACHACUTI
Incan emperor, 1438–1471
Wicked ways: the Incan emperor took the defeated Chanca leaders and stuffed their skins with straw and ashes. The scarecrow corpses were taken to a special burial ground and seated on stone benches. The stuffed arms were bent so that when the wind blew, the dead fingers beat the stretched skin on their bellies like drums.

IVAN THE TERRIBLE
Russian ruler, 1530–1584
Known for: being terrible. Ivan's enemy, Prince Boris Telupa, had a wooden pole driven into his body and hoisted up – he took 15 hours to die, talking all the while to his mother who had been forced to watch. His minister Founilov was dipped in boiling water then had cold water poured over him so his skin peeled off like a tomato. His enemy Prince Michael was accused of being a witch and sent to be burned. Ivan shovelled hot ashes from the fire over the dying man.

RANAVALONA I
Queen of Madagascar, reigned 1828–1861
Wicked ways: Ranavalona started acting evil at a very early age … then got worse. She married King Radama I when she was very young and poisoned him. Ranavalona took the throne after bumping off any rivals. She then had most of her family assassinated.

JOSEF STALIN
Russian leader, 1879–1953
Known for: probably the greatest killer in all history. Probably to blame for the deaths of 50 million people – most of them on his side! Stalin's secret police and army wiped out anyone who stood in his way. But he helped Britain and her allies to win World War II so no one said too much about his nasty little life. 'Winners' get away with it.

LUCREZIA BORGIA
Italian duchess, 1480–1519
Known for: Lucrezia is supposed to be one of the deadliest women ever to have lived. It is SAID that she wore a ring that was filled with poison. Her husband's enemies were invited to a meeting and she served them wine – then slipped in the poison. When adults drink wine they clink their glasses together. That is said to be an idea from the days of the Borgias. If a little wine slops from each glass to the other, it proves the other person hasn't put poison in yours.

MURAD IV
Ruler of the Ottoman Empire, 1612–1640
Wicked ways: Murad wandered the streets in disguise to spot troublemakers and then had them executed. Anyone caught drinking coffee or smoking was also executed on the spot. Smoking was definitely bad for your health when he was around. He once came across a group of women singing in a meadow and having a picnic. 'I hate that noise,' he said. 'Drown them in the river.'

MARY ANN COTTON
English killer, 1832–1873
Known for: misery Mary killed about 15 of her own children and three husbands. She poisoned the children with arsenic from a teapot. They all died a slow and painful death. She tried to have her last child taken into a workhouse but they refused to take the boy. Mary said… 'Never mind … he won't grow up.' The workhouse keeper said, 'He looks a healthy lad to me!' A week later the boy was dead.

ADOLF HITLER
German leader, 1889–1945
Wicked ways: Germany was in a mess after losing World War I and people wanted a strong man to lead them. Hitler had potty ideas but the Germans believed him. He said the Jews were to blame for Germany's defeat and the answer was to massacre them. And people believed him. Six million Jews were killed. Hitler lost the war and shot himself. No great loss; just a shame he didn't do it 20 years earlier.

Villains come in all shapes and sizes, from school bullies who will knock out your teeth for a bag of sweets, to 'great leaders' whose orders lead to misery for millions.

People from Herod to Hitler have made the evil rules. Hitler said 'exterminate the Jews' but it was other people who actually did it – them and millions of others throughout history. The 'ordinary' people. People like me, people like you, can be the most horrible of all.

There's no room for nice guys in Horrible Histories. Colour in the villains below instead. (See, I told you there were more.)

GENGHIS KHAN 1162–1227

Genghis Khan was the ruthless leader of the Mongol Empire. He has a nice motto you might like to follow: 'The defeated must die so the winners may be happy.' In other words, 'I'm not murdering you because I'm nasty – I'm doing it because it will make me happy.'

BLACKBEARD 1680–1718

Blackbeard was a pirate you would NOT want to see at sea or cross cutlasses with in a cabin. He sometimes killed his own crew for sport and wore plaits in his hair so it looked like snakes were crawling over his face and head. He even twisted smoking rope into these plaits to add to his terrifying looks!

DICK TURPIN 1705–1739

Dick Turpin was a butcher boy until he decided there was more money in stealing cattle than chopping them. He joined 'The Essex Gang' of violent housebreakers and became a horrid highwayman. They entered someone's home, robbed it and tortured the occupants till they handed over their money and valuables.

AL CAPONE 1899–1947

It didn't pay to upset old Al. One man who tried to steal Capone's business was 'Bugs' Moran. Al Capone set up a very special Valentine's Day gift for 'Bugs', then Al went on holiday to Florida. On 14 February 1929 Al Capone's gang dressed up as police and raided Bugs's hideout. As Bugs's gang put their hands in the air and threw down their guns, the fake cops machine-gunned them to death. It was known as 'The St Valentine's Day Massacre'.

ARTSWEEK EXHIBITION 2017

What can I say? Every year I think we can't do better than the one before - and then, here we are again. Just the quickest glance around the walls of the art room will show how successful we've been this year. So much great art, so many great artists and so many great styles. We've covered everything from cave painting to post war British architecture. I particularly liked showing off Year Two's hieroglyphics and Year Four's Aztec pictograms (once we'd removed the rude comments smuggled in by the Dutton sisters).

Other highlights were Hannah Turner's painting of Henry VIII as a monster, Aaron Kleck's working model of a Victorian privy, Kamal Hassam's 'Geek' statue and Eleanor Blatheringstone's rather elaborate drawing of a First World War carrier pigeon, representing the dove of peace, tangled and disembowelled by the barbed wire of no-man's-land - representing ignorance. I have to say I was a little shocked by this last picture but sometimes works of art are confrontational and challenging and worth a few tears - the odd scream - and a bad-tempered meeting with angry parents.

As you walk around the exhibition you'll notice work produced during some of our art trips from the year. We 'borrowed' the new time machine to do some live drawing of historical events. But since it is a time machine, we brought it back before we borrowed it. So, technically, it was never gone. I was keen for the Year Sixes to sketch Stonehenge as it was being built. Turns out Bronze Age local funding is much like our own and construction was halted halfway through. It's been that way ever since.

We also did an architecture trip — Norman castles in Wales — and a fine art visit inside Leonardo da Vinci's studio. Exciting sounding tours I'm sure you'll agree. However, those of you 'lucky' enough to be on those outings will know why we won't be doing any more. Mr da Vinci was not a particularly patient or understanding host and the Normans were downright nasty. Still, we escaped with some great sketches. I really like the one of William the Conqueror and his pet rabbit. Who knew?

But apart from the occasional hospital visit it's been a great year — or should I say years. This year marks my twenty-fifth in the department. And what a quarter century it's been. The results of our efforts in those early years have all grown up now. They might have been a bit unusual and 'rough round the edges' but they have gone on to do great things. And they're still as popular as ever. The little scallywags! Of course the department has grown. First Ms Shepard joined us, then Mr Reeve (now over at Creative Writing as you know). They were followed by Mr McDonald, Mr Phillips, Mr Davis, Mr Ford and Mr Smith. Quite a team. The whole school has grown. We now have a drama department and a multi-media studio where they've made radio and even TV programmes. We've got mugs coming out of the pottery shed and pencil cases from the Resistant Materials chaps in block D.

I'd also like to take this opportunity to thank Ms Scoggins and Mrs Daukes on the board of governors for their help and support. But most of all, a huge thanks goes to our handyman, Richard, without whom, we in the art department would not be able to sharpen a pencil. Everything would grind to a halt without you. Our work, like our pencils, would be pointless.

So — back to the exhibition. I hope you enjoy our collected works. Believe me when I say, if they are as much fun to look at as they were to do then I'll be a very happy art teacher indeed. Although 'enjoy' might not be the right word for Lucy Butler's effort. I think perhaps using real thumbscrews was a step too far.

Best wishes,

Martin Brown

Head of Art

TERRIBLE TRAVELS

Have you ever seen a film about pirates? They were funny old characters, and liked a good laugh and a quick chorus of 'Fifteen men on a dead man's chest, yo-ho-ho and a bottle of rum!' Then they battled bravely against huge Spanish galleons and made the cowardly captains cough up some terrific treasure. Right? Wrong. Here is the terrible truth about the gorgeous Georgian pirates:

SPANISH TREASURE SHIPS By Georgian times there were no Francis Drake characters attacking Spanish galleons and winning gold for England and the Queen. They attacked little trading ships to steal tobacco or slaves or just spare sails and anchor cable. ('Your anchor cable or your life?' doesn't sound so gorgeous, does it?)

HEAD-SCARVES Did they really tie large, coloured handkerchiefs round their heads? Yes. (If you want to try this then use a clean hankie. 'Snot very nice otherwise.)

WALKING THE PLANK Have you ever seen the play *Peter Pan*? Cut-throat Captain Hook plans to make the Lost Boys walk the plank and drop off into crocodile-infested waters. Very dramatic. But true? No. Pirates couldn't be bothered with that sort of play-acting. Some cruel pirates did tell their captives, 'You're free to walk home!' while they were in the middle of shark-filled seas. If they wanted to get rid of their victims then they just hacked them to death and threw them over the side. (That's a bit boring – especially for the victim, who'd be bored to death – but it saved a lot of time.)

MAROONING Did they really leave a sailor on some desert island with a bottle of water and a gun? Yes, they did. It was a punishment usually kept for pirates who tried to desert their shipmates. The most famous marooned sailor was Alexander Selkirk whose adventures were turned into the story *Robinson Crusoe*. (Imagine being alone and lonely with no friendly human to talk to. You'd go mad. And teachers are still doing this today. They call it detention.)

THE JOLLY ROGER FLAG Did pirates fly the black flag with a white skull and crossbones? Sometimes. Most Tudor and Stuart pirates flew a red flag – they put a story around that the flag was dyed with blood. Georgian pirates started to come up with their own designs. (What picture would you have on your flag to strike terror into the hearts of your enemies? A school and cross boys, perhaps.)

WOODEN LEGS Did pirates limp around on wooden legs? Some did. Fighting against the cannon of naval vessels was dangerous, and legs, arms and heads must have flown around like skittles in a bowling alley. Of course they didn't have doctors on board to make a neat job of a mangled arm or leg – but the ship's carpenter could carve you a neat replacement.

PARROTS Did pirates have parrots on their shoulders? Not usually – but they often carried them in cages back to Britain from South America. They could teach them to speak during the voyage back across the Atlantic then sell them as pets in Britain.

BURIED TREASURE Much more money has been spent searching for pirate treasure than has ever been found. If you won a million on the lottery would you bury it? No, you'd want to spend it. So did the pirates. Was there ever such a place as Treasure Island? The writer Robert Louis Stevenson spent a wet holiday in Scotland in 1881 and painted a map of an island for fun. He named it Skeleton Island and liked it so much he wrote the book *Treasure Island* to go with the map. Stevenson never met a pirate and he pinched the 'Dead man's chest' song from another writer's book.

TALK LIKE A PIRATE

Thinking of running away to sea on Blackbeard's boat?

If you don't want to be spotted as a lousy landlubber, you'll need to learn to talk like a pirate. Here are a few words to get you started...

AHOY 'Ahoy' means 'hello'. Most pirates aren't polite enough to use this word.

AVAST YE If you see a ship you want to capture you have to tell it to stop. Do NOT shout, 'Excuse me, but would you mind slowing down so I can rob you?' Shout 'Avast ye!' It means, 'Stop ... or else!'

AYE 'Yes'. You should say this to almost everything your captain asks you. Unless he asks, 'Did you steal the last of my biscuits, you bilge rat?'

AYE AYE 'I'll do that right away, captain.'

BILGE The very bottom of the ship. This is where water seeps in, rats live and all the filth of the ship ends up. It stinks and the air down there is deadly. Never call a pirate a 'bilge rat' or he may take a cutlass to your cheeky tongue.

HAIRY WILLY Dried fish. It might look disgusting, but it's better than nothing ... just remember you're eating something pirates call 'Hairy Willy'.

HEAVE TO Want a ship to stop? then call out 'heave to' – that means 'stand still'. It has nothing to do with 'heaving overboard', which is what you'd do if you found an enemy on your ship.

LANDLUBBER A 'lubber' is a clumsy person on a ship, who'd be happier on land. If you really want a cutlass up your nose, call a pirate a 'landlubber'.

SCURVY KNAVE Scurvy means mean, despicable and generally rotten or scabby. And a 'knave' is a villain. So scurvy knave or scabby villain: take your pick – or pick your scab.

SCUTTLE If you're in danger from attack by another ship, you may want to sink your own ship and row off in a lifeboat. Do NOT say, 'Poke a little hole in the boat and let it sink.' To sink your own ship is to 'scuttle' it.

SHIVER ME TIMBERS If a ship gets a sudden blast from a cannon then its masts ('timbers') are shaken (or 'shivered'). So a shocked ship has shivered timbers. If YOU get a shock then don't say, 'Goodness me, I am surprised!', say 'Shiver me timbers!'

SLOPS 'Slops' were the 1700s sailor word for trousers. Sailors were among the first people to wear them.

SWABBIE A 'swab' was a mop made of rope ends or threads. A 'swabbie' had the job of mopping the deck – cleaning up the blood and guts after a fight.

Vile Victorian Schools

So you have to go to school? Blame the Vile Victorians! In 1870 the Education Bill was passed. The aim was to: *bring education within the reach of every English home, aye, and within the reach of those children who have no homes.*

Now education was free for everyone. You had to go to school, whether you wanted to or not! You'd be caned if you didn't go – and probably caned if you did go. It was tough being a Victorian kid.

Children of the 21st century still suffer the horror of homework, the terror of teachers and the dread of school dinners. But, if you think school is bad in the 21st century, you should have gone to school in the 19th!

Foul Facts

1 Many parents couldn't afford to send their children to the new Board Schools set up in the 1870s. It wasn't just the penny a week they had to pay – it also meant that children weren't free to help their mothers with the housework, or earn the family extra money by working.

2 Some schools had special offers like, 'Three for the price of two'. If there were three children in a family at school, then the parents paid for the first two and the third could go free.

3 Some parents blamed teachers for making the children go to school. One teacher wrote...

I well remember how, early in my career as a teacher, I had to avoid various missiles thrown at me by angry parents who would rather have the children running errands or washing up things in the home than wasting their time in school with such things as learning.

4 If a parent didn't want to send their child to school, they would say that the child was ill. A School Board Inspector would have to go to check if the 'illness' went on too long. One inspector was told that a child was dead – when he visited the house he found the 'dead' child was so well she was skipping in the middle of the living-room floor!

5 School Board Inspectors were so unpopular in some areas that they had to go around in pairs – to protect each other from angry parents!

Some vile Victorian teachers didn't believe in talking to pupils to find out why they did something wrong. They simply punished them. Teachers had a motto...

"FOR BAD BOYS A YARD OF STRAP IS WORTH A MILE OF TALK."

6 The Victorians believed that boys should be treated differently from girls ... and that men were more important than women. This showed in the schools. In 1870, women teachers were paid 58 pounds a year ... but men were paid 94!

BOYS' LESSONS INCLUDED carpentry, farmwork, gardening, shoe making, drawing, handicrafts.

GIRLS' LESSONS INCLUDED housewifery (sweeping, dusting, making beds and bathing a baby), needlework and cookery.

7 There were often as many as 70 or 80 pupils in one class. The teachers would have to shout or even scream to be heard above the noise of the children. One doctor had so many teachers complaining of sore throats he called it, 'Board School Laryngitis'!

8 Punishments were given in factories to get the most work possible from a child. One man, Joseph Lancaster, invented a similar system of punishments which was used in some schools. (They are quite vile, so please don't try out on your teacher!) ················▶

THE LOG – A piece of wood weighing four to six pounds was tied across the shoulders of the offending child, when he moved, the log acted as a dead weight. It was punishment for talking, which often didn't work as the child would be in floods of noisy tears.

PILLORY AND STOCKS – Unlike earlier times, children who suffered this 'pleasure' were not pelted by rotten tomatoes. They were put in the stocks, left and forgotten about.

THE CAGE – This was a basket suspended from the ceiling, into which the more serious offenders were put.

MAKE THE PUNISHMENT FIT THE CRIME

Here are four school sins. What punishment would you give for each one?

1. Throwing ink pellets in class, punished by...
a) A severe talking-to by the teacher
b) Kneeling on the floor with your hands behind your head
c) A treble helping of lumpy mashed potato at school dinner

2. Missing Sunday church, punished by...
a) A severe talking-to by the priest and detention while you listen to the sermon you missed
b) A beating with a strap
c) Doing extra work for the church – polishing the candlesticks, digging a few graves, copying out the Bible, etc.

3. Being late for school, punished by...
a) Having your name written in the Punishment Book so you may not get a job when you leave school
b) Being hit over the hand with a cane
c) Both

4. Ink blots and fingermarks on work, punished by...
a) Being caned (so your hands are sore and you probably make even more mess)
b) Having to do the work again
c) Death

Now make up a putrid punishment of your own. What would the sin be and how would you be punished for it?

School sin...

....

Punishment..

....

Answers at the back of the book

WORLD WAR WORKERS

School is hard work. After you finish school, you'll finally have a chance to get a job and relax. Maybe you'll become a doctor (save lots of lives) or a teacher (ruin lots of lives) or a horrible historian (write about lots of lives – nasty ones). There were some lovely career options during the First World War, too. Which of these jolly jobs would you apply for?

VACANCY: SOLDIER

If you were a fit, single man over eighteen then you had to join the army whether you liked it or not. And there are many stories of boys going into army recruiting offices to join up even though they were under age. Many army recruiting officers were willing to let them join anyway. Of course it was their duty to check on the age and reject the ones who said they were under age. This story is true and happened hundreds of times all over the world.

RECRUITING NOW: SPY CATCHER

In the years before the First World War Britain was overrun with German spies because they guessed this war would come one day. It wasn't till 1908 that Britain had any spycatchers – the Secret Service Bureau.* Captain Vernon Kell was the only member of the Secret Service Bureau and by the start of the war in 1914 he had only nine officers. The Bureau did such a good job that they arrested 21 agents as soon as the war began.

Fancy joining them? Can you crack this German code? Match the code to the real meaning ... the simple spy men left enough clues in the choice of words.

1 Floating Down	**a)** Dartmouth Naval Base
2 Old folks at home	**b)** Destroyers
3 Dark Melodies	**c)** Old battleships
4 Chattanooga Rag	**d)** Southampton
5 Down South	**e)** Submarines
6 Pirates of Penzance	**f)** Chatham Base

Answers: 1e), 2c), 3a), 4f), 5d), 6b). How did you score? Down South = Southampton! Chattanooga Rag = Chatham. Difficult, eh?

* In 1916 this was renamed Military Department 5 – the famous MI5. By the end of the war it had 844 members.

WANTED FOR IMMEDIATE START: FIELD DOCTOR

Army hospitals in the First World War are better than they were in the Crimean War (1854–6). Nurse Florence Nightingale made things a little safer. Back in Florrie Nightie's day a wound could get infected – if the bullet didn't kill you then the germs did. But even in the First World War doctors can still be pretty clumsy. One Soldier reports...

> AN AUSTRALIAN SOLDIER, PRIVATE O'CONNOR, WAS WOUNDED IN THE LEG AND CAPTURED. HE WAS TAKEN TO ISTANBUL WHERE AN ARMENIAN DOCTOR OPERATED TO CUT OFF O'CONNOR'S LEG. THE DOCTOR SAWED HALFWAY THROUGH THE BONE, GREW TOO TIRED, AND SNAPPED OFF THE REST.

NEW POSITION: POLICEWOMAN

In July 1915, 30,000 women paraded in London under the banner, 'We demand the right to serve'. Women slowly began to take up jobs in war work, especially making weapons and ammunition (munitions).

Britain also created its first policewomen during the First World War and one of their duties was to stop women workers taking explosives out of the factories, and to stop them taking cigarettes or matches into the factories.

Policewoman Greta East kept a diary of her life on duty at a South Wales Munitions factory...

> 10 April 1917
>
> The girls here are troublesome about bringing in cigarettes and matches. Last week a woman came to the Women Police Office and asked me to rescue her coat from the cloakroom as she had a train to catch. She said I'd recognize the coat because it had her payslip in the pocket. But, when I searched the pockets I found them full of cigarettes. Of course the poor wretch had to be prosecuted and fined. She must have forgotten about them.

By the end of the war, 30 police forces had appointed women – another First World War idea that is still with us.

MARTIN'S
TOP 25 MOMENTS

DISCOVER ILLUSTRATOR MARTIN BROWN'S TOP 25 HORRIBLE HISTORIES MEMORIES.

1. To start at the start. The moment back in 1992 when the editor at Scholastic looked up at me from behind her desk and said, 'Hold that thought. Something's just come in I think you might be interested in.' I'd been illustrating a series for Scholastic called Coping With... and I was wondering if we could do a *Coping With... History*. But brighter minds had already been at work. Terry Deary's marvellous manuscript was on its way and editor Helen wanted me to do the cartoons for it.

2. The first editorial meeting with Terry, myself, Helen and Alison, the art director. I scribbled out some rough cover ideas for *The Terrible Tudors* and *The Awesome Egyptians* – and drew some words in a box that ended up becoming the Horrible Histories logo.

3. Realising that our little project of two books had become two more books and even more books after that. Then even more books after those.

4. Seeing the first copies of the foreign editions. How my cartoon jokes translated into so many different languages I will never know. By the way, Horrible Histories became Brutte Storie in Italy, Förfärliga Fakta in Finland, Hrôzostrašná Historia in Slovakia and Krrraupioji Istorija in Lithuania.

DON'T FORGET **FRENCH!**

5. Nerves jangling, doing my first Literary Festival event in Cheltenham in 1997.

6. Being invited to do an event at the Tin Tin exhibition in Newcastle in 1999. Even being in the same building as all that amazing Hergé artwork was an honour.

7. My Blue Peter Award. I say 'my' – it was actually Terry's Blue Peter Award – his second one – but he gave it to me. He's a very nice man.

YES I AM

8. Seeing the books in a little local bookshop near my parents' house – in Melbourne, Australia.

9. The Horrible Histories 10th anniversary party (and quiz).

10. The party in the Tower of London to launch the TV series.

11. The parties in the Imperial War Museums – North and South – to launch their Horrible Histories exhibitions. (I like parties.)

12. An example rather than a moment... Terry has always been such a brilliant writer to illustrate for that there's way too much terrific text to choose a favourite from. But out of the thousands and thousands of words I'll pick pages 42–3 from *Vicious Vikings* where Terry tells the tale of the Battle of Stamford bridge as if it was a newspaper story. It didn't need an illustration.

WHAT! NO PICTURE?

13. Visiting a school in a fairly deprived part of Glasgow and being blown away by the brilliance of the teachers and the buzzing enthusiasm of the kids. It looked like a prison from the outside but inside it was totally inspirational.

TUDOR THOUGHT IT!

14. Doing the drawings for the Horrible Histories: Specials series of books for *Scotland*, *France* and *The USA*. They're my favourites.

15. Finishing doing the drawings for *The Wicked History of the World* (now entitled *The Horrible History of the World*) our first full-colour book. It was done with watercolour, ink and pencil – unlike the lovely digital colour Rob Davis and Geri Ford do for the titles these days. It took AGES!

16. Not really one moment but many – meeting our fabulous readers at events and signings. Boys and girls, big and little, and littler. It's always a joy to speak to the real heroes of our success.

17. Being asked to be the illustrator in residence for the 2012 Bath Children's Literature Festival. Huge fun.

18. Drawing the little seal gag you can see in the middle of page 28. Stupid, but I like it.

19. The first time I saw those brilliant Birmingham Stage actors performing *Terrible Tudors*. And watching the Bogglevision cannonballs fly.

20. Then, years later, nerves jangling, again, being on stage with the Birmingham Stage Company with Terry, for their 10th anniversary gala performance.

21. The Scottish Book Trust children's book tour of Orkney and Shetland. It would have been hard work if it wasn't so much blinkin' fun.

22. Seeing and hearing the song 'Born 2 Rule' by the Four Georges from the first Horrible Histories TV series. I knew then that Terry and I could relax – the TV show was going to be a hit.

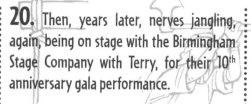

BY GEORGE!

23. And it was a hit – the BBC celebrated with a massive Horrible Histories Children's Prom in the Albert Hall. It was just extraordinary to see what those first few books had become.

24. A letter from a girl named Holly who loved the books and drawings so much she wanted to become an artist when she grew up. Mad fool.

25. Flying back to Australia for the National Maritime Museum *Horrible Histories: Pirates Exhibition*. It was a special trip. A lovely opportunity to share some of the Horrible Histories craziness with my family – and see the little pirate parrot blown up to five metres tall and overlooking Darling Harbour in Sydney.

Martin busy at work

No. I lie all the time! I like pretending I'm from Russia, and wearing disguises, too.

A SPY

You're brave, brilliant and born to serve your country. You travel into enemy territory and pass secrets back to your government. You're an ace at cracking codes, a master of disguise and you can speak lots of different languages. But can you hold up under torture? You'll have to if your true identity is discovered...

Yes. Liars should be locked alone in their rooms and fed bread and water.

A MONK OR NUN

You're more holy than your socks! You spend your life in the monastery (or nunnery) praying, working in the fields, helping the poor and needy, praying, sleeping in an unheated room, praying, eating foul mush, and writing books. (Tip for monks – want to know how to get the bald bit on the top of your head? Rub it with a stone.)

I tell him to bring his sister to my cottage, so I can cure her.

A WISE WOMAN

You're a very important person – people who can't afford to go to the doctor come to you instead. You cure people with herbs, and use the odd magic spell. But watch out – one minute people think you're a wise woman, then they're calling you a witch – and the next thing you know, you're being burned at the stake!

I report him to the authorities so he can be punished. Off with his head!

AN EXECUTIONER

You've got a good aim with an axe, a strong stomach, and you look good in black. You chop the heads off criminals (and people the king or queen just don't like very much). You don't have a very popular job, but don't worry, no one knows who you are – your name is kept secret, and you wear a hood so no one can recognize you.

A crow – I've got a head for heights.

A CHIMNEY SWEEP

Your job is perfect for children – you have to be tiny to fit up the chimneys. You work in hot, dark cramped conditions, cleaning away the soot from fireplaces, so it's too bad if you don't like small spaces or have asthma. Make sure you don't get stuck in the chimney or fall asleep on the job – your master will light a fire underneath you!

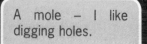

A mole – I like digging holes.

A MINER

Congratulations – you've got the dirtiest and most dangerous job of all! You work underground, digging up coal for 16 hours a day. If you think you're too young for a job like that, you're wrong – Victorian kids started working in the mines aged five. But watch out – a mining inspector said, 'Mining gives more ways of dying than any other job.'

BIG HORRIBLE HISTORIES EXAM

Here are twenty five horrible questions to celebrate twenty five horrible years!

1. What is a Stone Age barrow?
a) A Stone Age device with one wheel, used for carrying dead animals
b) A Stone Age farming tribe
c) A Stone Age burial place

2. How did ancient Egyptian embalmers remove the brain from dead pharaohs?
a) They stuck a hook up the nose and pulled the brain out through the nostrils
b) They sliced open the top of the head and removed the brain with a special spoon
c) They sucked it out through the ears using a straw

3. This sacred plant was once sprinkled on to graves. But we don't consider it sacred today. What is it?
a) Parsley
b) Cabbage
c) Garlic

4. The Romans didn't have tomato ketchup but they did have sauce made from what?
a) Sheep eyeballs
b) Fish guts
c) Elephant's tails

5. Romans fought and raced in an 'arena', which was full of sand. The word 'arena' meant 'sand'. Why was there sand in the arena?
a) To soak up all the blood
b) So it was soft for fighters to fall on
c) So fighters could pick up a handful and throw it in an enemy's eyes

6. Rome was able to grow to be a great city because of its sewers. How big were they?
a) Big enough for a man to crawl through
b) Big enough for a 12-year-old boy to walk through without bending
c) Big enough for a horse and cart with a load of hay to drive through

7. What was the name of the largest Celt tribe that fought the Romans?
a) Celtics
b) Gauls
c) Zulus

8. There were no prisons in your local Saxon villages. Fines were easier to arrange. Which of these crimes must you punish with a fine, your honour?
a) Eating meat on a 'fast' or holy day
b) Making a sacrifice to a pagan god
c) Unlawful marriage

9. As well as using mud, the Saxon also slapped a rather more nasty substance on the walls of their houses to plaster them. What is it?
a) Chicken's blood
b) Pig's poo
c) Sheep's earwax

10. Vikings used 'kennings' or word-play. So a 'horse of the waves' was a ship. What was 'the sweat of the sword'?
a) Rust
b) Blood
c) The handle where the warrior placed his sweaty hand

11. What was the Norman punishment for murder?
a) Hanging by the neck till dead
b) Having your eyes put out
c) Beheading (with a blunt axe)

12. If you go to a wedding today then you may throw confetti over the bride for luck. In the Middle Ages the guests threw...
a) Grains of rice
b) Tins of rice
c) Sawdust

13. In 1337 Edward III claimed to be King of France. The French disagreed and the Hundred Years War started. How long did it last?
a) 15 years
b) 100 years
c) 116 years

14. In Inca society, there were three main crimes that you could be punished for: murder, insulting the emperor and insulting the gods. The punishment for these was death and the Incas had a simple way to execute someone. What was it?
a) They would cut the criminal to pieces and feed them to the guinea pigs
b) They would drown the criminal in Lake Titicaca
c) They would throw the criminal off a cliff

15. What did Inca women use to hold their hair in place instead of hairspray?
a) The juice of fruit
b) Their own wee
c) Water

16. What sort of knife did Aztec priests use to cut out a victim's heart?
a) Glass
b) Bronze
c) Gold

17. Henry VIII died on the morning of 28 January 1547. For the next three days what curious thing happened?
a) One by one his faithful dogs died of broken hearts
b) Henry had all his meals served as usual
c) The money that he kept in his room disappeared mysteriously

18. What was the speed limit for London coach drivers in 1635?
a) Thirty miles an hour
b) Three miles an hour
c) Twelve miles an hour

19. In 1788 six shiploads of convicts arrived at Port Jackson in Australia. 570 men and 160 women stepped ashore. Of these first convicts the youngest was how old?
a) Nineteen
b) Fifteen
c) Nine

20. Where would rich Stuart people get false teeth from?
a) Carpenters made wooden ones
b) Potters made china ones
c) Poor people sold their good ones

21. Georgian highwaymen couldn't always afford pistols. In 1774 a Huntingdon highwayman held up a coach using what?
a) A bow and arrow
b) A savage dog
c) A candlestick

22. In 1875 the first one was opened in London. First what?
a) Roller-skating rink
b) Ice-skating rink
c) Bottle of ink

23. The Gloucester hangman liked to show off at public executions to give the crowd a laugh. What did he do?
a) He tap-danced on the scaffold while the crowd waited for the prisoner to arrive – a bit of a jig
b) He wore a black hood over his head but put false hair on top of it – a bit of a wig
c) He let the victim drop, then twirled the rope – a bit of a pig

24. The women who worked with TNT explosives in World War I were nicknamed 'canaries'. Why?
a) They were so happy they sang like canaries while they worked
b) The TNT caused their hair to turn canary yellow
c) Because the factory owners were getting 'cheep' labour

25. If you didn't have an air-raid shelter in your garden during World War II, where was the best place to go in London to beat the bombs?
a) The Underground
b) The Tower of London
c) A boat on the River Thames

PENS DOWN!

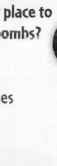

Answers at the back of the book. (No cheating.)

55

AWFUL ANSWERS

p.15 The 'Doctor! Doctor!' Quiz

1a) Yes – eating cooked mouse really was a 1920s' cure for bedwetting. In Egypt the bones of the mouse were NOT eaten but wrapped in a cloth and the cloth hung round the neck of the child.

2b) Animal liver is high in vitamin A and could help some types of night-blindness.

3b) Medicines were made from all sorts of poo – from fly droppings to ostrich poo.

4b) Honey was put on the wound and probably worked in a lot of cases. It is an antibiotic (so the Egyptians made a lucky guess), but they believed that evil spirits hated honey and would be driven off by it. (Not such a good guess.)

p.19 Spot the Lot

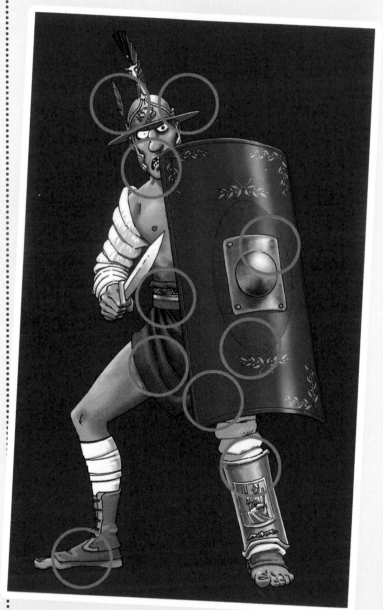

AWFUL ANSWERS

p.32-3
Where's Rattus?

p.47 Putrid Punishments

1b) Kneeling
One punishment was to kneel on the hard, rough floorboards, with your back upright and your hands placed on the back of your neck for a long period of about twenty minutes. Should you lop over, aching all over, the teacher would slap you across the head with his hand and shout sternly, 'Get upright, will you?'
- Victorian boy

2b) The strap
Every Monday morning the priest came to each class and asked us who had missed church the day before. I always had to miss Sunday because Sunday was washing day and we only had one lot of clothes. So, week by week we admitted our absence and were given the strap for it. We should have been able to explain but we were ashamed to give the real reason. Once, just once, I answered back.

'Don't you know,' the priest said, 'that God loves you and wants to see you in His house on Sundays?'

'But if he loves us, why does he want us to get the strap on Monday?' I asked.

I don't remember what the priest said, but I do know I got a double load of stripes when he'd gone.
- Victorian girl

3c) The punishment book
With no exams at the end of your school life, the chance of a good job after school depended on your final report – your reference. One boy was kept back by his father and so he was late for school... The only boy in the school to be late.

I was humiliated in front of three hundred boys by the headmaster and afterwards got six mighty slashes on the fingers with a thin cane. My God, it hurt, believe me. And something else which hurt even more. My name was inserted in the disgrace and punishment book and put on record for future reference.
- Victorian boy

4a) The cane
Some teachers chose especially thin canes because they hurt more. Many a time the cane would be broken over the hand (or bottom) of the pupil. Caning still went on in English schools more than eighty years after Victoria died (ask your grandparents!)

57

AWFUL ANSWERS

p.54-5 Horrible Histories Exam

1. c)

2. a)

3. a)

4. b) The guts were soaked in salt water and left to stew in the sun for a few days. Then the fish-gut sauce was poured over the food as a tasty treat. Oh my cod!

5 a) The sand soaked up the blood – sometimes. But after very gory fights or animal massacres there were slaves sent in to scatter fresh sand. Still, the rotting blood must have smelled pretty awful.

6. c) In 33 BC the Roman General Agrippa had them cleaned out. Agrippa was also an admiral of the navy. His greatest boat trip was to sail through the sewers to check they were clean.

What a way to check a job. That's what's called 'thorough'. Still from time to time, the sewers did get blocked and the forum was flooded with sewage. You'd have to hitch up your toga and paddle through poo.

7. b) Roman Ammianus Marcellinus noted that the Gauls were fierce, argued a lot and were proud.

8. a) b) and c) These were all fined.

9. b) Pig poo – it's versatile, tough and super-smelly!

10. b)

11. b) The Normans were cruel but they rarely gave the death sentence to criminals. Prison was only used to hold criminals until their trial. A murderer might lose his hands or his eyes. Having your eyes put out was also the punishment for killing one of William the Conqueror's deer. Does that

mean a human life was worth no more than the life of a deer?

12. c) Rice is an Asian crop not grown in England. If any did reach Britain in the Middle Ages then it would be far too precious to waste on a buxom bride! ('Buxom' meant 'obedient' because that's what a Middle Ages woman promised to be.)

13. c)

14. c)

15. b)

16. a) The knives were made from a type of natural glass that came from hardened volcanic lava. It is called 'obsidian' and can be polished to look really sharp, shiny and attractive. It's used to make jewellery now.

AWFUL ANSWERS

17. b) Henry's death meant the country was without a leader until young Edward's protector could sort things out. Enemies could have attacked while England was leaderless. So foreign visitors were told, 'King Henry VIII is a little poorly but he's still eating well.' Then Henry's meals were carried up to his room with an escort of blasting trumpets. Not even the loudest trumpets would wake the old corpse and it's for certain he didn't enjoy those meals! (But his hounds probably did.)

18. b) Of course there were no policemen with speed traps – but if a coach overtook a walking law-officer he could face a fine.

19. c) John Hudson was a nine-year-old chimney sweep. He must have felt a bit lost, poor kid! After all, there weren't a lot of chimneys in Australia in those days. He'd have to get a new job – kangaroo-pouch-sweep, maybe?

20. c) 'If a gentleman has lost his teeth there are dentists who will insert into his gums teeth pulled from the jaws of poor youths.' – Advert, 1660

21. c) The candlestick may have looked like the barrel of a pistol but the guard on the coach wasn't fooled. He shot the highwayman with a blunderbuss gun and two slugs ended up in the thief's forehead. The candlestick robber was snuffed out. He probably got on the guard's wick.

22. a) Roller skates had been invented over a hundred years before but this was the first 'rink' to be built. Back in 1760 skates were worn by Joseph Merlin to a musical party. He skated into the ballroom, playing a violin Sadly he lost control, skated into a £500 mirror, smashed it, smashed his violin and almost cut himself to shreds.

23. c) Not only did he spin the corpse on the end of the rope, he also slapped it on the back and shook hands with it. He pretended to have a chat to it and all the audience were laughing.

24. b) TNT caused nasty skin rashes and its fumes turned the girls' hair and skin bright mustard yellow – the colour of canaries. These unfortunate girls were often refused service in restaurants whose owners said, 'You are unsightly. Go away because you are putting the other customers off their food!'

25. a) People snuggled down on the platforms at night. It wasn't very comfortable at first, but later they put in bunks for people to sleep on! Also useful for a quick kip if your train was delayed…

Brand new! ↘

HORRIBLE HISTORIES
TOP 50 KINGS & QUEENS
TERRY DEARY MARTIN BROWN

HORRIBLE HISTORIES
TOP 50 VILLAINS
TERRY DEARY

HORRIBLE HISTORIES
LONDON
Get the whole GORY STORY of LOATHSOME LONDON
TERRY DEARY MARTIN BROWN

HORRIBLE HISTORIES
FEATURING HOUSES
"I'm the ghostess with the mostess"
GRUESOME GREAT HOUSES
Terry Deary Martin Brown

HORRIBLE HISTORIES
CRUEL KINGS AND MEAN QUEENS
Terry Deary

HORRIBLE HISTORIES
"I hate the knight shift"
DARK KNIGHTS AND DINGY CASTLES
Terry Deary

HORRIBLE HISTORIES
"He's a real knight-mare"
ENGLAND
Terry Deary Martin Brown

HORRIBLE HISTORIES
IRELAND
Deary Martin Brown

HORRIBLE HISTORIES
"Alive alive"
GRUESOME GUIDE TO DUBLIN
Terry Deary

HORRIBLE HISTORIES
With HORRIBLE Highlights MAP
"I'm Mad Dan McKill and he's my best friend"
GRUESOME GUIDE TO EDINBURGH
Terry Deary

HORRIBLE HISTORIES
With HORRIBLE Highlights MAP
"He's got a degree and he's got a pedigree"
GRUESOME GUIDE TO OXFORD
Terry Deary Martin Brown

HORRIBLE HISTORIES
With HORRIBLE Highlights MAP
"GRRR!"
GRUESOME GUIDE TO YORK
Terry Deary

HORRIBLE HISTORIES
With HORRIBLE Highlights MAP
"This is the place to be"
"We're all here to make little sacrifices"
GRUESOME GUIDE TO STRATFORD UPON-AVON
Terry Deary

HORRIBLE HISTORIES
FEATURING CASTLES
"I'll crack you up"
CRACKIN' CASTLES
Terry Deary Martin Brown

HORRIBLE HISTORIES
"I've got a mammoth's brain"
SAVAGE STONE AGE
Terry Deary Martin Brown

HORRIBLE HISTORIES
"Tomb service..."
AWESOME EGYPTIANS
Terry Deary & Peter Hepplewhite Martin Brown

HORRIBLE HISTORIES
"It's all Greek to me!"
GROOVY GREEKS
Terry Deary Martin Brown

HORRIBLE HISTORIES
"I get the point!"
ROTTEN ROMANS
Terry Deary Martin Brown

HORRIBLE HISTORIES
"We're all here to make little sacrifices"
CUT-THROAT CELTS
Terry Deary Martin Brown

HORRIBLE HISTORIES
"Bloomin marvellous"
SMASHING SAXONS
Terry Deary Martin Brown

HORRIBLE HISTORIES
"It's not the x-factor!"
VICIOUS VIKINGS
Deary Martin Brown

HORRIBLE HISTORIES
"It's knight time."
STORMIN' NORMANS
Terry Deary Martin Brown

HORRIBLE HISTORIES
"You've got to have heart!"
ANGRY AZTECS
Terry Deary Martin Brown

HORRIBLE HISTORIES
"Inca stinks."
INCREDIBLE INCAS
Terry Deary Martin Brown & Philip Reeve

HORRIBLE HISTORIES
"Knight knight."
MEASLY MIDDLE AGES
Terry Deary Martin Brown

HORRIBLE HISTORIES
"It's ruff at the top."
TERRIBLE TUDORS
Terry Deary & Neil Tonge Martin Brown

HORRIBLE HISTORIES
"Penny for the guy?"
SLIMY STUARTS
Terry Deary Martin Brown

HORRIBLE HISTORIES
GORGEOUS GEORGIANS
Deary

HORRIBLE HISTORIES
VILE VICTORIANS
Terry Deary Martin Brown

HORRIBLE HISTORIES
"I'm going up in the world!"
VILLAINOUS VICTORIANS
Terry Deary Martin Brown

HORRIBLE HISTORIES
"Cruel Britannia."
BARMY BRITISH EMPIRE
Terry Deary Martin Brown

HORRIBLE HISTORIES
"There's a stench in the trench."
FRIGHTFUL FIRST WORLD WAR
Terry Deary Martin Brown

HORRIBLE HISTORIES
WOEFUL SECOND WORLD WAR
Terry Deary Martin Brown

HORRIBLE HISTORIES
"The Blitz is the pits!"
BLITZED BRITS
Terry Deary Martin Brown & Kate Sheppard